the
you t   out

bente benedict

the stars you forgot about copyright ©2020 by
Bente Benedict. All rights reserved.
No part of this book may be used or reproduced in
any manner whatsoever without written permission
except in the case of reprints in the context of
reviews.

ISBN: 978-1-7003-4468-7
independently published with special thanks to
amazon kindle direct publishing
for making this possible

15th of December 2018, 22:34

instead of doing
a bit of light reading
i chose to do
a bit of light writing
today

however,
opinions differ
on how "light"
is defined as.

- and there the book was
  written

15th of December 2018, 22:25

love is paradoxical
opposing
contradictory

it breaks
and heals
it hurts
and satisfies

but isn't that
the most beautiful thing
about love ?

15th of December 2018, 22:50

snow
ice
hail
rain

what's the difference, really ?

it all started the same
it all will end the same
it is just in different forms
based on the situation it is in

asians
swedes
italians
americans

what's the difference, really ?

we all started the same
we all will end the same
we are just in different forms
based on the situation we are in

- some thoughts on equality

15th of December 2018, 22:55

selfishness
is survival
and the fatal fault
simultaneously

- paradoxes

16th of December 2018, 23:26

falling in love
is like drifting asleep

it happens
both consciously
and unconsciously
at the same time

16th of December 2018, 23:38

how can the universe
be an infinity ?

how can the amount
of stars in the sky
be infinite ?

when we
mere humans
are not capable
of understanding
even the complexity
and greatness
of one sheer planet ?

17th of December 2018, 00:05

we make art
through language

we communicate
in a way
only we
can understand

even though
we are speaking
the same language
as everybody else

we can understand
each other's
thoughts
feelings
intentions
by a sheer remark
or moment of eye contact
nobody noticed

and i think that is
a most wonderful thing

      - if only we'd realized it

17th of December 2018, 00:06

poems
are a way
of connecting
humans and
the enlightened

they make you think
but not too intensively

17th of December 2018, 00:10

i should never
have let you go
if only i'd known
what pain
it causes me now

    - regret

17th of December 2018, 00:19

i am at the point
where i don't care
if he's laughing
with other girls

if he still loves me
deep inside him
if only a tiny piece
of his love for me
is still left in him
i can survive

- our relationship ended years ago

17th of December 2018, 00:20

some nights
i just want to sleep

but both
my heart
and brain
keep spilling out
these poems

17th of December 2018, 00:30

i like how waves
can be

rhythmic and random
approaching and backing away
simultaneously

but i do wish
that people were
a little less
like waves
sometimes

17th of December 2018, 23:25

i am so confused
am i in love with you
or with the story
we used to have ?

17th of December 2018, 23:28

your smile
still gives me butterflies

your eyes
still remind me of the ocean

i am still longing
for the feeling
of your lips on mine

but i know
that it is over
and that i need
to move on

17th of December 2018, 23:30

if there would appear a star
every time i thought of you
it would explain
the infinite amount
of stars in the sky

17th of December 2018, 23:33

i know that it is wished from me
to say that i have moved on
erased you from my thoughts
left our history in the past
and that's what i'll answer
if someone asks

but honestly,
no matter how hard i try
i have not moved on
and never will

17th of December 2018, 23:51

a crackling fireplace
a dinner
that's already been prepared
a hot bath
after a long day

but most of all,
your smell
and
your warmth
on my cold skin

      - what coming home feels like

19th of December 2018, 00:06

i wonder
every now and then
how opinions
can differ so much

what i think
is a beautiful colour;
complementing the skin,
giving a tone of warmth

but what you think
is a disgusting colour
like rusted chains
so bitter and cold

even though we are seeing
the exact same colour
only through different lenses
that form our opinions

19th of December 2018, 00:08

why are you holding on
to things you don't have
anymore ?

that's what i ask myself
when i'm missing him
and i'm clinging on
the sweet memories

but still i can't formulate
a decent answer
to my own question

19th of December 2018, 00:11

possibilities are endless
but also limited

because there's an infinite number
of different colours
that can be combined
but still
only some will complement each other

and because there are billions
of people on this earth
that can be matched
but still
only a few fortunate hearts
will find the right match

19th of December 2018, 00:18

how biased memories can be
when love has touched them

when in love
the memories seem
sweeter
more peaceful
more innocent
and happier

but after the break-up
the memories will seem
so blinded
so unrealistic
and far from the truth

because
remembering
good things that have ended
will hurt more than
remembering
bad things that have ended
in the former we find regret
in the latter we find peace

20th of December 2018, 19:12

i still keep thinking
that one day
he'll come back to me
and that he'll say
that he never stopped
missing or loving me
and that we will live happily ever after

but life is not a fairy tale

20th of December 2018, 22:54

music is such a wonderful thing
it can be
loud
soft
subtle
hard

it magnifies our emotions
and finds a way to our souls

21st of December 2018, 22:53

are you familiar
with the feeling
of not knowing
where you are ?

not concretely though
because you could
mark your location
on a map

but just not knowing
what your place
on this earth
is really ?

- lost

21st of December 2018, 22:57

they say that
jealously
is a bad thing
something
to be ashamed of
when you're feeling it

however
i think that it is
an emotion
most essential for
"the getting over him"
and needed to close off completely
or re-bloom any relationship

21st of December 2018, 22:59

how sweet
lovely
alluring
these words sound
when they're coming
off your tongue
when it's your vocal cords
producing the sound of them

and then we're not even taking in
the content of the words
themselves

- the art of speaking

22nd of December 2018, 23:08

i know
it would be better
if i would just let you go
if i just stopped caring
about you

but i should leave out
the word "just"
because how on earth
do you do such a thing ?

22nd of December 2018, 23:13

distance
is such a weird concept

because even though
someone may be standing
a metre away from you
physically
they can seem
so far away
like they are wandering
off to a different world
in their minds

so i think
there has to be made
a distinction
between the distance
physically
and mentally;
between them
there may be
a world of difference

22nd of December 2018, 23:19

i love the way
our text messages
make me feel
like you're not
on the other side
of the world

like you're with me
here
now
not only in my mind
but also in
that remote universe
we created
for ourselves,
the one only we
can enter

22nd of December 2018, 23:28

sometimes
you're just not feeling it
and that's okay

sometimes you just don't have
a reason to get out of bed
and you don't have to

because those moments
will only be
a good moment of realisation
of what important is
and what isn't
and it will teach you
what to let go of
and what to hold onto

as far as i'm concerned
these downfall moments
are way more valuable
than most people may think

22nd of December 2018, 23:32

these nights

i know he's flirting
with other girls
and he can do so
as he pleases
our relationship
has ended some time ago
he moved on

and i am here
just me and my phone
in bed
late at night
writing these poems
some of them emotional
others just thoughtful
all of them a way
to release my thoughts

and sometimes that hurts me

but then i realise
how many steps
i am ahead of him

22nd of December 2018, 23:40

books are like magic
i've thought so
since i was a child

books occupy your time
without you realizing it
and without giving you
the feeling
that you've wasted your time
books stretch your knowledge
unknowingly
books take you to a different world
where you are left with the story
and your mere, vulnerable self

they make you
think
feel
experience
and
discover

after reading a good book
it feels like you experienced
the story in another life
and i think that is magical

22nd of December 2018, 23:47

there is this thing

professors don't teach you
at school
and that's not taught
by your exes either

it is something essential
that you should learn
from yourself for yourself

- self-love

22nd of December 2018, 23:49

remember
that your body
and mind

need rest
at different hours
and for different durations

23rd of December 2018, 23:21

oh how you
make my brain go
fuzzy
foggy
frantic

i love it though

23rd of December 2018, 23:24

i sometimes wonder
at what point
the amount of water drops
are too many to count
individually
and become a puddle

and at what point
the single occasions
we shared together
became a story

24th of December 2018, 09:29

you wish me a happy life
without you

but how is that even possible
when you are the reason
for my happiness ?

24th of December 2018, 22:22

me you can't fool
you know why
i simply know you too well
way too well

26th of December 2018, 14;22

is there someone
on this earth
that could help
my desperate heart
that is longing for love ?

- hope is all that is left

27th of December 2018, 23:30

is it possible
to have a triangle relationship
by texting ?

i think so
because you are
texting both her and me
and she knows it
and i know it
but we keep texting you
anyways
preferring to share you
over not having you at all

    -   divided attention

28th of December 2018, 22:44

patience
is something
i usually have
quite much of

but when it comes to you,
i cannot wait a single second
for you to text back
and
i cannot wait a single second more
to be in your arms again

30th of December 2018, 22:45

they say
you need to be feeling
complete
when you're single
first
before diving into a relationship
but how is that possible?

i used to feel complete by myself
when i was single
but then i met you
and it was like i was augmented
with a part that represented
you

that part has been taken away now
so at that place
amongst others
is where i feel the incompleteness
you left behind

so how do i make that hole
disappear
and how will i heal and feel
complete
by myself ?

30th of December 2018, 22:46

sometimes
i just need to
pour my heart out
get it off my chest
free my mind from the thoughts

that's where the poems come in

1st of January 2019, 00:29

the one thing
that is broken
more often
than hearts

is new year's resolutions

1st of January 2019, 22:20

sometimes
you just need to
take a moment
to relax

just breathing in
and breathing out
slowly
naturally
and reflecting
on all the hustle and bustle
that's called life

just take a step away from it
for a moment
look at it from a distance

your mind will find peace
that's a promise
from me to you

- meditation

2nd of January 2019, 00:20

oh how i confess my feelings
to you
so easily

it should be forbidden
what you do to me

2nd of January 2019, 23:22

next time you think of me
don't think about the past
because that's what i do
way too often

please
be more clever
than i am
and think of
the present
and the future

2nd of January 2019, 23:39

sometimes
when your name drops
in a conversation
or when we're texting
and i'm laughing out loud
about something you said

my parents look at me like
oh still that boy ?

and i will answer
in my head

*yes
it will always be
that boy*

3rd of January 2019, 22:53

please
take a moment
every day
to appreciate
the good things
in life

because a grateful heart
is something very valuable
to have
and makes you
more complete
as an enlightened human being

3rd of January 2019, 23:00

success
is something
worth working for
but it is not something
worth losing yourself in

4th of January 2019, 22:59

how beautiful
life could be
if only
we'd recognise
the good things
and appreciate them

- gratefulness

4th of January 2019, 23:12

whenever i'm feeling
dreamy
i surround myself
with flowers
because they remind me
of the sweetness in life

6th of January 2019, 23:56

discipline
is one of the most
precious qualities
a human can
possibly have

because if you have
so much strength
to control yourself
unconditionally
you can do almost anything

- willpower

6th of January 2019, 23:57

allow yourself to take time to grow
rome wasn't built in a single day

7th of January 2019, 22:30

you cannot just
destroy the planet
without expecting
any pain back

- thoughts on pollution

8th of January 2019, 22:22

are you familiar
with the feeling
of just floating in the sea
on your back
looking at the clear sky ?

i think it is one of
the most wonderful feelings
just floating and meditating on
whatever is on your mind

it is one of the feelings
most like liberty
and i love it

8th of January 2019, 22:30

i truly adore
the way
your eyes laugh

the little universe
i see in your eyes
makes my heart
just so very happy

9th of January 2019, 23:01

i honestly just adore
the way our fingers intertwine
your heat on my cold skin
the electric current
racing from
the tips of my fingers
to the tips of my toes
the feeling of safety, security

i actually just love everything
about holding hands

10th of January 2019, 22:54

nervosity
is something
almost no-one
can control

it captures you
and it controls
your mind and body
and i know how
powerful
such a sensation
can be

to conquer it
try breathing in and out
but i know
it's easier said than done

- tra il dire e il fare c'è di mezzo il mare

10th of January 2019, 22:55

your dashing smile
makes me so happy
in every single cell
of my body

11th of January 2019, 22:55

oh how feelings
towards certain people
can change
so abruptly
and irrevocably

12th of January 2019, 23:09

the most vague
and confusing
position
you can be in
is the one
between friends
and lovers
because you know there's more
than mere friendship
but you can't label it "love"
yet

so what is it exactly ?

12th of January 2019, 23:13

humans will always search
for a type of kick
they just like the feeling
of adrenaline flowing
through their veins
they seek adventure,
something new

in you i certainly found a kick
you made the adrenaline flow
you were an adventure
you were something new
but still i'm not sure
if it was really
the thing i was seeking

12th of January 2019, 23:16

although you can search
you will not always find
but if you don't search at all
you don't even have
the chance of finding

- optimism

13th of January 2019, 22:46

late night conversations
are the best

i sometimes have the pleasure
of texting a person
i feel quite attached to
at a rather late hour
and what i really like
about those conversations
at those late hours
is that you can feel
a very close connection
to this person
and your minds
become one;
it feels like you're in another world

or maybe this is all
just caused by my liking
for this person i'm texting

13th of January 2019, 22:49

please understand
that my brain
can't function
properly
when you're that

doing what ?
just that

smiling at me
laughing
talking

but worst of all
flirting
because then
my brain
just doesn't know
how to control itself

13th of January 2019, 22:51

attention
makes all things
richer

14th of January 2019, 19:40

nature
is so conflicting

it is
prepossessing
charming
ravishing
stunning

and
demolishing
shattering
devastating
threatening

simultaneously

15th of January 2019, 22:46

the senses
are so magical

the taste
rich chocolate
fresh pastries
crisp vegetables

the sound
first steps in fresh snow
waves approaching
a crackling fireplace

the feeling
sun rays on skin
floating in water
wind through hair

the smell
mowed grass
homemade apple pie
fresh bed sheets

the view
stars in the sky
sunsets on summery days
snorkelling above coral reef

- midlife miracles

17th of January 2019, 13:41

i am grateful
for everything life throws at me

the good things
because
they learned me
that life is
a wonderful adventure
and we should be
grateful for it

but also
the bad things
because
they shed light
on the good things
and make us
enjoy them more
and make you ready
to fight for
whatever you
want to achieve
in life

17th of January 2019, 13:50

i am human

i am vulnerable
i am strong

i can hate
i can love

i have talents
i have flaws

i can control my feelings
i can burst them out

i am selfish
i am noble

i am human

- balance

17th of January 2019, 22:57

being broken up with
is heart-breaking
we all know that

but don't underestimate
the pain
that is caused by breaking up
with someone you still love

because from experience i can tell
that breaking someone's heart
is more than heart-wrenching

18th of January 2019, 23:49

how often
can you actually
fall for someone ?

because every time
i see you
i'm falling for you
all over again

18th of January 2019, 23:53

imagine
a world without us

it would be
terrifying

18th of January 2019, 23:55

i don't know
how it works
exactly

but when it comes
to him
my patience
is limitless

and that's so stupid of me

20th of January 2019, 22:16

story time

i once got into a relationship
with a boy
now my ex

i broke up with him
not because i didn't love him
anymore
nor because he didn't love me
anymore
i just felt like he deserved better
but we all make mistakes

i broke his heart
and by breaking it
i broke mine too

regret is such a painful thing
that i experienced

but jealousy shouldn't be
underestimated either

he got a new crush
and i felt devastated

because i knew
i ended his love for me
love he now gave to another girl
who happened to be my friend
in the past
not anymore really
because i can't stand
them being together
seeing them
laughing
flirting
and her sitting on his lap
while they aren't even in an official
relationship yet

and this is what i did to myself
why am i so sadistic ?
i didn't do it on purpose, though
but i do know
that i need to practise self-love
for eternity
to make up for this
with myself

20th of January 2019, 23:46

this is so ironic
me trying to cheer you up
from the disappointment
another girl gave you

and me apologizing
for not being good at it

28th of January 2019, 22:25

what is reality, really ?
is it the things we see

or something else
out of our grasp
something ideal
that is happening
in the big black hole
that we call
the cosmos ?

and what if
the things we see
are just mere
representations
of the real reality ?

- conversations with plato

28th of January 2019, 22:27

fascinating
how our minds
so different
but so alike
have the tendency
to think about
the same things
at the same time

4th of February 2019, 22:14

how can i be
so in love
with everything
you do ?

every
thing

4th of February 2019, 22:14

oh what those
piercing blue
ocean eyes
do to
my sanity

insane

4th of February 2019, 22:15

i'm never not thinking of you

4th of February 2019, 22:16

why is it that
everything you do
catches my attention ?
interest me ?
preoccupies me ?

4th of February 2019, 22:20

why is it that
sometimes
i'm all you're interested in
and sometimes
i don't catch your attention at all ?

i wish i could be that good
at balancing out

4th of February 2019, 22:36

in one way or another
the last thought i have
when drifting asleep
always is you

- how can i help it ?

5th of February 2019, 23:03

self-love
is the most pure
form of love
a human being
can experience

6th of February 2019, 22:31

close your eyes

the darkness represents
what i'd feel if you'd leave me

- but i know you won't

6th of February 2019, 22:32

trust
is something
that should be earned
through time
it should be valued
when received
it should be treated
with extreme caution
because it can be taken back
at any given moment

6th of February 2019, 22:36

some people can be
so cold
while their temperature
is high

10th of February 2019, 22:17

love can conquer everything

every
single
thing

10th of February 2019, 22:43

i like balancing things out

some days
i'll be eating
a bucket of ice cream

other days
i'll be working out
intensively

that's the beauty in life
the yin and yang

- equilibrium

11th of February 2019, 21:43

how different
our worlds
may be

we belong together

11th of February 2019, 22:58

your love
is like an elixir of life to me
i need it to survive
when you gave it to me
every day
i was satisfied

now i am thirsty
my mouth is dry
longing for your sweet liquid love
but i know you will never
give it to me again

so i must wait
till every cell of me
has dried out

11th of February 2019, 23:04

our love is horizon broadening
without having to travel

11th of February 2019, 23:07

the way you look at me
gives me chills
and heat waves
at the same time

- fever

12th of February 2019, 22:12

boy
i invented you

i made you how i wanted you to be
without realizing you didn't need
making; you were already a whole
but perhaps not made for me

- in my head

17th of February 2019, 22:15

you were a hurricane
extraordinary
chaotic
wild
reckless

but most of all
destroying

17th of February 2019, 22:17

every now and then
i catch myself gazing blankly
out of the window
so why is it always
when my mind drifts off
that i'm thinking of you ?

- daydreams

18th of February 2019, 13:10

life is an act of balancing out
the negative and the positive things

let the positive ones outweigh

18th of February 2019, 22:15

late at night
when i'm trying my best to fall asleep
and while i'm waiting for the dreamy
feeling to overwhelm me
and lead me to the peaceful, quiet
place we enter when we are asleep
where all is sunny and calm

is the moment you again come to
occupy my thoughts

- and 2 hours later i was still wide awake

19th of February 2019, 22:00

it may not seem like it
but we are all enslaved
there is one slavery
that we all take part in

we are slaves of social media
we are slaves of other's opinions
we even are slaves of ourselves
because you can push yourself
to do something
because your mind says
it is the best to do
but thereby you are
enslaving your heart
that does not want to do it

so what is freedom in reality ?
remarkable is that seneca
had an answer to this:
he said that you should not
see yourself as a slave;
not feel mentally limited by it
and slavery will become worthless

but i know this can be
a hard thing to do
and not everyone
is into stoic philosophy

19th of February 2019, 22:01

i am scared
scared to make this sprouting
relationship bloom
scared to put it in fertile soil
scared to let the sun rays heat it;
supplying it with the healthy and
necessary vitamins it seeks
scared to give it the attention and time
it so desperately needs in order to rise

scared to put the water with the roses

19th of February 2019, 22:34

poetry is something
that just comes and goes
like waves

you can't sit down at a desk
and tell yourself to write poetry
for an hour or two
it wouldn't work
because the inspiration comes
from little everyday things

a poem will randomly pop into your
head
and you have to write it down
in order to keep it

it is infrequently and unexpectedly and
i love it

26th of February 2019, 23:23

even though
you feel like
you will never
get over him;
i know you can

picture your love for him as a rose
if you give the rose the sun and water it needs,
it will grow to a beautiful flower
if you don't give it any water;
it will die eventually

so gotta keep the water away from it
if you want to get over that boy

26th of February 2019, 23:26

i'm in love with being in love with you

26th of February 2019, 23:29

oh how i envy
the ones who've
already found
their true love
and are living
happily ever after

i've always wanted to be a princess
but i never knew why
now i know it was not
because of their dresses
it was because of their princes

26th of February 2019, 23:33

as innocent children
we never knew
how complex
understanding
four letters
would be

- love

27th of February 2019, 23:28

i loved you unconditionally

but i had not taken in mind
that you loving me back
was a condition

28th of February 2019, 22:42

patience is all it takes
after that we can dive right into it

3rd of March 2019, 11:20

sometimes
the things that are right in front of us
take us the longest to notice

4th of March 2019, 21:47

home is where you feel most yourself

6th of March 2019, 09:16

infinity can be temporary

6th of March 2019, 09:24

the moment your lips touch mine
gravity becomes non-existent

9th of March 2019, 23:17

your body
lying so close to mine
radiating warmth
and giving me comfort
your hug is a safe hiding place
from all the bruteness in the world

it's the place where i will always want
to be

9th of March 2019, 23:22

you once told me you loved me most

but was it the most
you were capable of
or was it the most
you thought
you were capable of ?

- but then you met her

9th of March 2019, 23:23

women don't need makeup to feel pretty

they need to find their true selves and then the confidence will come

11th of March 2019, 22:41

as infinitely stretching as the universe
is my love for you

11th of March 2019, 22:48

curious
how you and i met so innocently
not knowing how huge the roles we'd
play in each other's lives would be
nor expecting us for a moment to fall
in love so recklessly and so deeply

had we known it in advance,
would you & i have still been strangers
now ?

11th of March 2019, 22:55

in self-defence
i tell myself over and over
to stop loving you

but i simply find myself to be
incapable of that
whenever i try
so i guess i will just love you
with all i can
until i can no more
that will be my end
isn't that loyal ?

11th of March 2019, 22:57

as dark as a cold winter's night are my thoughts towards her

- good luck with your new girlfriend

11th of March 2019, 22:58

our love story was like a lovely
summer's day;
warm but freshened by a gentle breeze

but i forgot to mention
that after every summer
the cold and dark, wintry nights follow

12th of March 2019, 22:08

*"can true love for someone
ever fade away totally,
as if it had never existed ?"*
you wonder

my answer: *"no, if you spill a drop of
paint on a white sheet, what would
happen ? it can spread, it can fade
away, but never cease to exist, just
like true love"*

12th of March 2019, 22:10

you were so unpredictable
never foreshadowing
what you were going to do next;
and yet boys still claim to be
easy to read

13th of March 2019, 22:32

i want you to look at me
the way i look at the stars
while sitting in my window sill at 3 am

13th of March 2019, 22:35

the stars give me so much inspiration
even though some of them
might have ceased to exist already

weird to think about it, admiring
something that doesn't exist anymore
in reality
while you'd think it still does

perhaps just a little like our love

17th of March 2019, 22:30

please know i still worry about you

how are you ?
everything okay ?
anything on your mind ?
something you need
to get off your chest ?
just anything, really

i just feel the constant urge
to check up on you
i miss you
and i'll be there for you
always

18th of March 2019, 22:44

oh what it is to be alive
and in the thrill of it all

20th of March 2019, 21:50

what were you up to,
stealing my heart ?

20th of March 2019, 21:52

me: *lying in bed, trying to fall asleep*

my brain: oh hello there, so what will we think about for the next coming hours ?
your ex or how we should stop climate change and all the other problems in the world ?

me: none of them please, i'd like to go to sleep

my brain: all right so let's do both then, we'll start with your ex

20th of March 2019, 21:54

were we meant to be not meant to be ?

20th of March 2019, 22:00

hours, days, weeks, months
we texted at night
about all the deepest things imaginable

and now it's hard for you to even say
"hi" to me when we're passing in the
corridors

23rd of March 2019, 22:40

while waking up in your arms i always wonder whether i'm still dreaming or not

23rd of March 2019, 22:41

you claimed i was hard to read while
i was an open book

open your eyes, you will discover a lot
more about me than searching for the
blind spots with your eyes shut

28th of March 2019, 16:48

thinking about not thinking
is still thinking

- oh teach me how i should forget
 to think

1st of April 2019, 16:32

life continues
even though it might seem
as if it won't
the world hustles on

21st of April 2019, 00:05

i should have known
that true love is
a priority above everything

should have known it
when i was wasting
your precious love
with prioritizing useless things
which i then thought to be
more important

25th of April 2019, 18:55

in another universe
you & i will meet again
and we will start all over

1st of May 2019, 21:58

why is it
that i still care for you
so much
while i am perfectly aware
that you don't care about me
at all anymore ?

1st of May 2019, 22:00

some emotions are simply
too complicated
to give them a label

7th of May 2019, 20:54

they say that a billion futures
lie ahead of us,
and only one will happen in real life
every choice we make leads us to the
one future that will become the reality

now i ask; did i make the right choices
to have ended up in this future ?
was it meant to be this way
or did i make a wrong choice ?

- fate

11th of May 2019, 14:04

some people are so active
in being passive

17th of May 2019, 17:22

where can we find motivation
if not in ourselves ?

17th of May 2019, 17:34

for more than a year i've been friends with my ex now
it sounds peaceful, but trust me: it is not

it is nice that we just have to say half a word to each other and know what we mean, that one glance at the other is a conversation itself, for that our eyes can speak

yet it is tough, to be friends with a boy i still adore in a way, seeing him look at his new crush, a girl who used to be my friend

and since we are crystal clear about everything, i know for a fact that he likes her, he confessed it to me after i told him my suspicions
i knew he liked her before he even knew it himself
but i also know that deep inside he will never lose a small piece of his love for me nor will i for him, that he knows too

it is a difficult situation, but i know
i can't stand being less than friends

i'm scared of what the future will
bring, but still i hope
he will be a part of it
and, god, how i wish him a happy and
fulfilling life, like he deserves, either
with or without me in it

- whatever is best for him

17th of May 2019, 17:37

watch out not to drown
in the ferocious river
that is called a busy life

21st of May 2019, 16:39

what's in a name
many may ask

still i do think
that sunday
is the best day
of the week

21st of May 2019, 16:41

people can seem so possessed when
earning money is what they're striving

how i wish they could be that
motivated when it comes to
fighting global warming

21st of May 2019, 21:56

daily i wonder

why did i
stupid as i was
let that boy
who loved me so thoroughly
and enriched my world so
go ?

26th of May 2019, 09:27

strength is proudly showing
your vulnerabilities

26th of May 2019, 09:27

my love for you is as infinite as the numbers behind the comma of pi

- 3,14159265358979323846264338327950288419716939937510
....

26th of May 2019, 09:27

revenge always ends up
to being a vicious circle

26th of May 2019, 09:27

being scared
is not being able
to control
your fantasies

3rd of June 2019, 18:15

we are living a deceptive truth
but when is something deceptive ?
when is something truth ?

the fact that we might never know
implies
that we are living a deceptive truth

7th of June 2019, 22:19

please never ever ever make the
mistake
of reading back text conversations
from you and your ex

never
 ever
 ever

17th of June 2019, 20:27

some days
i am just in desperate need
of chocolate
in order to maintain
a sane state of mind

    -   please understand that

17th of June 2019, 20:29

a million things to do
and only so little time

 - why can't we freeze the hourglass ?

17th of June 2019, 20:32

don't y'all feel it
starting from the beginning of june
when the first rays of sunlight
have kissed your skin
the twinkle in your stomach
that it is slowly arriving,
the one thing we have been waiting for
the whole year ?

- summer

17th of June 2019, 23:50

when waking up every day
the dawning realisation
like a knife that's stabbing me
that i messed it up
that i wasted his love for me
and that i can never fix it again
nor rewind the time to when
our love was still blooming
it just hurts like heaven

- dead flowers remain dead

17th of June 2019, 23:52

tu sais que je t'aime
he said
and only this could have been enough
for me
to learn french

18th of June 2019, 21:15

i adore
that you
adore me

18th of June 2019, 21:15

so many people see each other
without really seeing them

18th of June 2019, 21:16

did i love you,
love that i loved you or
love that you loved me ?

18th of June 2019, 22:46

no victorian age novel will describe
cheesy enough how i feel about you

4th of July 2019, 23:12

is it human
to feel our emotions
so magnified
or am i just an alien ?

5th of July 2019, 23:36

he is everywhere

from the high school
we went to together,
the classrooms still a memory
of me and him holding hands
during the lessons,
whispering words
into each other's ears
trying not to get caught talking
during class

to the bicycle stands,
where he asked me
if i wanted to be his girlfriend
and where i gladly said yes,
not knowing how life changing
that decision had been

and my house,
where he liked to come to
and where we'd sit
talking in the garden
or taking stupid selfies in my room

my driveway,
where we were standing to say
goodbye
when he had to go home
and where he gave me
a kiss on the cheek
for the first time

and the house in portugal i stayed at
that summer holiday,
while he was home,
texting and calling me every day,
asking how my day had been
while i was sitting on the stairs there
the only place with wi-fi,
looking at the same stars
he was looking at,
listening to his velvet voice
coming out of my phone

pieces of him are everywhere,
for most invisible,
only to us tangible
because of the memories
we have there
he is everywhere

10th of July 2019, 23:32

i sincerely hate the version of me that
lived in the time when he loved me,
for not realizing how blessed i was
with a boy who was so captivated by
me and devoted all his love, time and
attention to me

right now, i'm thinking about how
grateful i am
for the relatively short time
i spent with him
and how grateful i am for having been
a small part of that boy's life
while knowing and mourning over the
fact that i probably am too late forever

1st of August 2019, 21:39

i am at the point now
where i can sincerely say to myself
that i am happy for him
to have found a girl
he is so happy with,
and so excited about
whenever they
are making progress
in their relationship
even though that girl is not me

and if that's not progress
in the getting-over-him-process,
nothing is progress

4th of August 2019, 12:21

i'm missing the feeling of missing you

*because feeling a need
towards someone
however painful that may be
is still better than
not feeling anything
towards that person
at all*

4th of August 2019, 12:21

i keep forgetting to forget you

22nd of August 2019, 18:46

<u>a recipe of things i need
to distract me from you</u>

some days, everything i need is my
italian lover who whispers things
like *tesoro*, *carina* and *amore*
in my ear

other days, i need my bestie with me,
who knows me better than
i know myself and with whom
i can laugh over all the things
we've been through together

some days i need a girls night
with my sisters, watching movies
and eating popcorn

and again other days, i just want a cosy
night with my mother, drinking tea
and eating chocolate

20th of August 2019, 09:57

i'm hoping on hoping for you

5th of September 2019, 14:08

i used to think all boys
were kinda like him
that how he was to me was normal,
because that's how all boyfriends act,
right ?

now i realize it was just him
who was like that
i took him too much for granted
and i didn't realize how grateful i
should have been for such a boyfriend
but i just didn't know that other boys
were so *different*

he was my first
my first real one
i couldn't compare him
to a previous one
i couldn't have known

now i can compare him
and realize that he really was
one of a kind

if only he hadn't been the first

6th of September 2019, 07:44

four starred hotels are not about the
big, fluffy, comfortable pillows
they're about the fact that the pillows
have the hotel's logo embroidered on
them

think about that as a metaphor for a
second

10th of September 2019, 17:46

people emotionally heal
in the way flowers grow

they first need to come back
to their senses
plant their feet in the ground
they need to root

then there comes the caring part
let the sun shine on them
surround them by sunny souls

give them some water
nourish them
chocolate will always do

and lastly, have patience
and attention for them
it will take some time
flowers don't grow overnight either

11th of September 2019, 17:48

he was exactly the definition of
extraordinary

as if that word
was made specially for him
tailored and all

as if they knew
the word "unordinary"
simply would not do
to describe
such a human being

11th of September 2019, 18:02

how ironic it is
time takes away
all the dear things from us
but creates life-changing
opportunities on its way

11th of September 2019, 18:03

deep inside us
we are all just lost poets
wandering
wherever our hearts will take us

11th of September 2019, 20:40

he was the hot shower after a rainy day
he was the steamy cup of tea
the comforting armchair
the bar of seventy five percent
dark chocolate
the classical victorian age novel
the oversized hoodie
the sound of a relaxing nocturne
played on a pianoforte

he was everything that made a wintery
day less dreary

13th of September 2019, 15:38

god could be a woman
why exclude the possibility ?

i know i am saying this as a woman
but i am not particularly being a
feminist here

it's just that i've always liked
the idea of
defying the basic standards

18th of September 2019, 22:34

yes, he has had other women
before he met you
that's a fact you can't change
so don't try to make him
forget the previous ones
let him remember them
but be so ravishing
that the previous ones
cease to be of any relevance

18th of September 2019

why does our society weigh so much
importance on the "firsts" ?
first boyfriend. first kiss. first job.
don't the following ones
have any extra significance ?
isn't the fact that you proceed
after the first time just as important ?
and the last ones.
aren't they noteworthy either ?
aren't we curious about why it ended ?

- fervently scribbling down these words at 2 am. the whole country is asleep. and dark. the only light coming from my bedside lamp. the only sound coming from my fine liner, writing on a fresh page. questioning things that are seen by society as "normal"

18th of September 2019, 22:42

at one point
i felt so whole
so complete by myself
that i just didn't need
a man in my life
i was enough

but then that lover walked
into my life
so unexpectedly
feelings grew so rapidly
that now,
i am addicted to manly attention

- is that a sin ?

18th of September 2019, 22:45

those holidays
feeling the summery breeze
in your hair
walking in the sea with your bare feet
tasting the salt on your lips
hearing the ocean at all times

we want to dwell on those moments
forever
that's why most people take
a little something from that place
to remind them of those happy,
careless times

i am bringing home the sun
carrying it on my skin
with a tanned touch to it

yes, i know, the caramel colour will
fade away eventually
that's why i will have to come back
next year

- temporary souvenir

18th of September 2019, 22:47

the moment
my head touches my pillow
intentionally going to sleep

my mind becomes a universe
an infinitely stretching space
with an unknown
and unpredictable amount
of solar systems
carrying thoughts
and for the majority
far-fetched and
out-of-the-blue ones

20th of September 2019, 18:26

and as the world dies
they will wash their hands in
innocence
but nobody will be left
to remember
that humans
were the blame to all of this

- global warming

27th of September 2019, 14:28

an infinity
of things
to think about

and
my mind
wanders
back
to you

27th of September 2019, 17:17

why is it that
we only miss
something
once it is gone ?

is it because
we are so used
to the presence of it
that we only realize
how dear
it was to us
once it is absent ?

9th of October 2019, 22:28

the day your smile was taken away
the earth mourned with me
the clouds cried their hearts out
the winds wearily wept and
the flowers drowned themselves

my hand stopped writing
my pen ran out of ink and
my tears blurred my written work
i tore it apart, for it was worthless now
it didn't exist anymore

you regained your smile - fortunately
i am still searching for mine though

13th of October 2019, 12:54

how sad it is
to look in the mirror
and see the eyes
of a stranger
staring at you

- changed forever

15th of October 2019, 22:05

he was the first one
to look behind my façade
to dare unravel the mysteries
rooted deep inside me

and i'm grateful
because after him
i opened like a flower
that had seen the sun
for the first time

16th of October 2019, 18:59

it is
understandable
that you do not
understand me

16th of October 2019, 19:09

tell me,
is she playing her part well
does she know her lines or
does she improvise too much

is her voice honest
when she says *i love you* or
is her tone all wrong

are her facial expressions okay or
is that spark in her eyes absent

is she the actress you need
to distract you from me or
is the movie too cliché to watch ?

19th of October 2019, 23:09

forever torn
between
memories
and
future possibilities

19th of October 2019, 23:19

i keep finding myself
chasing paths
i chose not to choose

20th of October 2019, 01:33

my parents think
i'm blind
to love him
but they
don't understand
i'm not blind
on the contrary
i see in him
what they cannot

25th of October 2019, 19:05

strangers stared at me
while i was going for a run today
who is that girl ? their eyes asked
why is she running here so confidently
where does that faint smile
playing around her lips come from
doesn't the wind exhaust her;
her cheeks are blushing, why ?

but they couldn't have known
that i felt as if i'd been reborn
they couldn't have known
that once again,
i just felt so utterly myself

31st of October 2019, 17:40

we could have been everything
that young love is
we could have been loved by
and in love with each other
in a way that makes outsiders blush
we could have been like the victorian
age novels or like romeo and juliet
without the tragic ending

something in your eyes tells me
we could have been star crossed lovers

if only they weren't there,
the stars you forgot about

we've arrived at this point
the end of the story - for now

he and i parted long ago
he has got a new girlfriend
i have got a new boyfriend
the "us" he and i used to be
only exists in the past
and in our memory
because i will never forget
and i know he won't forget it either

sometimes something small
seeing something
particular in his eyes
takes me back to that time
and then i realize that
love felt so different with him
so different than it feels now

so, for the last time
i will let the words
in my heart spill

love,
come back to me,
if you too feel like maybe,
we were meant to be

quickly getting out of the shower
after having made a poem in my head
waking up after a dream
reading particular words or
feeling particular emotions
that feeling after
contemporary dance class
where you're meant to spill feelings of
desire and loss – thinking of you

our short but unforgettable story

- writing the book

dear reader

*thank you. every single one of you.
for spending your precious time
reading the book i wrote when i was
sixteen. i cannot tell you
how grateful i am. like any writer
i hope my words changed you.
me they have changed. i am different
now. thank you for that. i needed the
change. maybe you needed it too.
you're welcome. it was a pleasure.
and trust me, something new is
coming. i am never at rest.
always a work in process.
this story has not ended yet.*

- see you in my next book

Printed in Great Britain
by Amazon